Credit Repair
Made Easy

Guide to improve your life with better credit!

Ra'Shawn D. Flournoy

Credit Repair Made Easy

ISBN: 978-0-578-24423-5

Dedication

Dedicated to my loving mother Alice Tanner & grandmother Gloria Flournoy. Love and miss you both so very much!

Disclaimer

This book has been written for information purposes only. Every effort has been made to make this eBook as complete and accurate as possible. However, there may be mistakes in typography or content. Also, this book provides information only up to the publishing date. Therefore, this eBook should be used as a guide - not as the ultimate source.

The purpose of this book is to educate. The author and the publisher do not warrant that the information contained in this book is fully complete and shall not be responsible for any errors or omissions.

The author and publisher shall have neither liability nor responsibility to any person or entity with respect to any loss or damage caused or alleged to be caused directly or indirectly by this book.

This book offers financial and legal information and is designed for educational purposes only. You should not rely on this information as a substitute for, nor does it replace, professional financial or legal advice.

Table of Contents
Credit Repair Made Easy

Introduction

Most people don't understand the credit system that well. All they know is it determines whether or not they'll get approved for a loan or credit card. But what they don't know is how to repair their credit after it has been damaged.

Not paying your bills is only part of the reason why your credit score gets lowered. The immoral and deceptive practices of creditors do a lot to ruin your credit as well. That is why you must understand everything there is to know about the three main credit bureaus and how their computer systems calculate your credit rating and manage your credit records.

This book was written to educate you on the entire credit system and how to improve your credit. After you make it to the end of this book, you'll have a clear understanding of how credit scores are calculated and how they can be changed for the better or worse. This includes how to file a dispute with the credit bureaus if you find errors or discrepancies in your credit report.

As you progress through the book, you will find template letters for requesting the removal of inaccurate information from your credit report. You can send these letters to the appropriate credit bureau along with your dispute form. If the credit bureau approves your request, your credit score will be updated with the correct information added.

All the steps to help you understand the credit system and repair your credit are laid out in this book. When you put this information into action, you'll end up with a superb credit rating once again. Then you can apply for bank accounts and loans as needed.

Chapter 1 – Why Good Credit Matters

When you apply for credit, and your application gets approved, it establishes an agreement between you as the borrower and the financial institution as the lender or creditor. The agreement states that you agree to repay the amount you borrowed under the terms of the contract signed. These terms include things like interest rates and term limits.

Banks are the most common lenders because they are in the business of issuing loans and profiting from the interest charged on them. But other types of companies can be lenders, such as car dealerships, credit card companies, student loan agencies, personal loan agencies, and mortgage companies.

Lenders won't issue loans to just anybody, though. They'll want to review your credit history to see if you're trustworthy when it comes to fulfilling your financial obligations. If you have a history of paying your debts without falling behind, you'll be considered a low-risk applicant. Then your application will likely get approved.

It is essential to focus on the repayment terms of the loan contract. Even if you get approved, it doesn't mean the terms are perfect. Your credit profile can still influence your interest rate and loan term limit. A better credit history means you'll have better repayment terms with a lower interest rate.

Remember that lenders can charge almost any interest rate they want. Credit cards and personal loans, for instance, could have an APR of 80% to 90%. That means you'd be paying back almost double the loan amount because of the added interest.

For this reason, you need to take your credit seriously. Nowadays, you can lose more than a loan opportunity if you have bad credit. Employers are starting to reject job applicants for having bad credit scores too. It's kind of strange because how is somebody supposed to pay their debts if they cannot get a job? But that's the way it works now.

Whenever you owe money to some person or company, it can influence your credit. Your payments to insurance companies, credit card companies, mortgage companies, utility companies, and even cell phone carriers will keep your credit high. But if you were to miss just one payment to any of these companies, your credit rating could be set back for years.

A bad credit rating can almost feel like a jail sentence. It ruins your chances of purchasing a home, buying a new car, and getting hired for a job you're fully qualified to perform. Does this seem like a good enough reason to take your credit profile seriously?

An Overview of Bad Credit

Thousands of people have credit problems because they cannot afford to pay off their debts. Some people cannot even afford to make the minimum monthly payments to their lenders. This causes the borrowers to end up owing more money because of all the interest charges and penalty fees that get added to the principal balance.

Did you know that over 50% of Americans have less than $1,000 saved? The reason is due to all the money they owe creditors. No one can save money under these conditions. Interest rates have skyrocketed on loans, and it seems like creditors can charge whatever they want now.

The sad thing is that many people don't understand how much their outstanding debt affects their credit rating. They usually figure the debt will get paid after their financial circumstances change for the better. But the reality is that bad credit can prevent you from improving your life and getting out of the hole you're in.

Think about this as an example. Let's say you have bad credit and cannot afford to purchase a car to get to work. How will you ever get to work and fulfill your daily responsibilities if you don't have a car to drive around? It's not like you can take the bus to go everywhere. And even if you could, buses cost money too.

The best solution is to repair your credit as early as possible. It might force you to take out a car loan with a much higher interest rate and higher monthly payments. Auto lenders will judge your car loan terms based on your credit score and overall credit history.

If you already have a good credit score, you can expect a low-interest rate and a longer-term limit, which means you'll have low monthly payments. But if you have a bad credit score, you'll have a higher interest rate and a shorter-term limit, which means your monthly payments will be higher.

Car Loan Scenario

Suppose you have good credit and get approved for a $15,000 car loan at a 5% interest rate for 72 months. Your monthly payments will be approximately $242. At the end of the 72 months, you would have paid $17,424 in total. That is an extra $2,424 in interest payments.

Now let's suppose you have bad credit and want to purchase the same $15,000 car. Well, the auto lender might approve your loan, but with an interest rate of 15% for 60 months. It would make your monthly payments approximately $357. At the end of the 72 months, you would have paid $21,420 in total. That is an extra $6,420 in interest payments.

Subtract $2,424 from $6,420, and you pay $3,996 in additional interest costs if you have bad credit. It is merely one example of why people with bad credit have more debt. Even if you make all your monthly payments on time, it doesn't matter. The terms of the loan are set in stone until you make all the payments.

What to Do?

High-interest rates make it so difficult for people to repair their credit. It is like a never-ending sea of debt that you cannot control. You could make your minimum monthly payment and still end up paying significantly more than you originally owed. And by the time the payment term on one loan is finished, you might have taken out another loan somewhere else that needs to be satisfied. The chain of debt lasts forever.

It is no wonder why so many American families live paycheck to paycheck. The average American family cannot even afford a $500 emergency expense. What does that tell you about how bad credit ruins people's lives? One emergency expense could become a long-lasting debt for many years to come.

If you take out a personal loan to cover the emergency expense, you'll have to pay more money in interest. It would be so much better if you had savings because you could use that to pay off the emergency expense without any interest being owed. But if you have no savings and bad credit, you're in a terrible financial situation.

The Bad Credit Bubble

Are you caught in the bad credit bubble and forgot how you even got there in the first place? It can feel like a never-ending cycle of moving forward and making payments on your debts while remaining in the same place financially.

First, do not panic because many people get trapped in the same type of bubble. The American financial system is designed to keep people in the bubble without any easy way out.

You might have had outstanding credit for most of your life. Unfortunately, it only takes one bad situation for your excellent credit history to get ruined.

A lost job or one emergency expense could be enough to send you into financial hardship. The experience will seem surreal because everything that was once good is now bad.

If you want to know another sad fact, most people stay in debt forever for one reason or another. Some of them cannot escape poverty and simply end up owing too many different creditors. What's worse is that predatory lenders seek financially desperate people and offer them high-interest loans, which only put them in deeper debt.

If people are desperate enough for money, they will sign up for those high-interest loans. Life never seems to slow down, even when you slow down. The downward trend usually begins after one late payment or one emergency expense. Your credit immediately becomes jeopardized, and the stress builds quickly.

As the bad credit bubble grows more prominent, your loan and credit card opportunities diminish. If you have any current credit card accounts, your credit limits will be set to a lower amount. The lower your credit score, the lower your credit card limits.

You might think a lower credit limit will prevent you from overspending on a credit card, but that won't necessarily be the case. There is something called an overdraft, which is when you spend more money than your credit limit allows. If you have an overdraft, you're charged expensive overdraft fees. Desperate people with low credit limits are more likely to overdraft because they need money.

If you must contend with overdraft fees on top of the interest charges and loan debts, it'll continue to grow your lousy credit bubble. Your credit score will then decrease as you struggle to make the monthly payments on all your credit accounts. If any of your loans have variable interest rates, you can be sure the creditors will increase them as a penalty for late payment.

Check the terms of your loan agreement. Sometimes the creditors are not allowed to increase the interest rates, especially if it's a fixed interest rate. But there may be other terms and conditions, which include late fees and adverse credit reporting. With each late payment that you make, it means one more negative mark on your credit report. Each negative mark will decrease your credit score quickly.

People don't typically find out how bad their credit is until they need it the most. That is why they're so susceptible to high-interest loans during times of crises. Just the fact that you're educating yourself on the whole credit system means you'll be vigilant about loan offerings if a crisis strikes your life.

But what if you don't have a choice but to take these loans? Many people live paycheck-to-paycheck and feel pressure to take high-interest loans to pay their bills during hard times. If you can turn things around for yourself now, then you can prevent yourself from getting to this point in your life.

The Value of Good Credit

Have you always dreamt about purchasing a luxury car or electric vehicle? It would certainly make you feel rich if you were to purchase a high-end car. But do you need to be rich to purchase one? If you have good credit, you can purchase a luxury car with a loan just like any other car.

Imagine being able to make your dreams come true by purchasing a 2020 Porsche Panamera for $425 per month. No car dealership expects you to pay the full price of the car in cash. They would prefer that you obtain a loan because the dealership and the lender can profit from the interest payments. All you need is good credit to get approved for such a loan.

What poor people don't understand about rich people is that they spend money on credit too. The difference is rich people can afford their monthly payments without struggling whatsoever. And they don't purchase these luxury items because they're necessities to them. Instead, these are items purchased for pure pleasure and vanity.

If you care about the American dream and all that it stands for, you'll need good credit to make it a reality for yourself. Good credit can earn you a loan for your dream home, higher credit lines on your equity, and higher limits on your credit cards.

Have you ever heard of wealthy people who have unlimited credit on their credit cards? These are people with a long and successful history of paying off their massive debts without missing any payments. That is the power of making payments on time and keeping your credit score high.

Rich people can usually get approved for credit cards with no more than a 3% interest rate. Since creditors trust rich people who have good credit histories, they don't need to charge them high-interest rates. They trust the payments will be made on time.

Lenders prefer clients with good credit histories because they're less likely to default on their credit accounts. It is the same with mortgage companies, banks, credit unions, and car dealerships. People with good credit are always treated better than people with bad or questionable credit.

In other words, someone with good credit will be offered better deals on loans than people with bad credit. You'd think it would be the other way around because people with bad credit don't have a lot of money. And yet, those people are the ones who have to pay higher interest rates. It doesn't make any logical sense.

However, if you think about it from the lender's perspective, they are running a business and need to make money. A rich person doesn't necessarily need a loan, so they wouldn't take out a loan if it has a high-interest rate. Only people who are desperate for a loan will do that, which would be poor people. That is who the lenders really make money from.

You don't need a million dollars in your bank account to be considered rich. If you have good credit and a stable income, you are already considered rich

by society's standards. Therefore, your primary goal should be to focus on establishing a good credit score rather than making a million dollars.

Chapter 2 – Understand Your Credit Profile

Do not assume your credit report is 100% accurate. The creditors who report data about your credit accounts to the credit bureaus are not always accurate in their reporting. If there is an inaccuracy or discrepancy in your credit profile, it could have a vastly negative effect on your credit rating.

How often do you check your credit report? You are entitled to one free inspection of your credit report per year. Unfortunately, most people don't take advantage of this opportunity. They will go years without checking their credit reports. But that is a bad thing to do because inaccuracies in a credit profile could be holding you back from a better job or bigger loan.

Everyone has a responsibility to know what is in their credit profile. You may request your credit profile from any of the three main credit bureaus in the United States. They are required to follow various state and federal laws pertaining to the handling and distribution of credit reports.

According to the Fair Credit Reporting Act, the credit bureaus must investigate any credit disputes filed. If you discover a piece of information in your credit report that you believe to be false, you must file a dispute with that particular credit bureau and explain the problem to them.

Their investigators will review your dispute to see if it is valid. If they determine it is valid, the inaccuracy will be removed from your credit report, which will ultimately affect your credit score for the better.

Creditors must similarly follow state and federal laws too. The only difference is they aren't required to validate the data they report to the credit bureaus. That is the responsibility of you as the credit account holder.

The Three Primary Credit Bureaus

The three primary credit bureaus in the United States are Equifax, Experian, and Trans Union. They are also referred to as CRAs, which stands for Consumer Reporting Agencies. There is a fourth credit bureau called Innovis, but most creditors do not even bother reporting to it. Only the first three credit bureaus are essential to them for reporting purposes.

If you attempt to retrieve your credit report from any of these credit bureaus, make sure you retrieve it from them directly. There are third-party companies that gather consumer information and sell it to consumers who want to see their own information. Don't waste your money on that because you can get your credit information from the credit bureaus for free.

Let's explore the different credit bureaus available.

Equifax

In 1898, Equifax was created by two brothers named Guy Woolford and Cator Woolford. It was the very first credit bureau ever to be established. Since its creation, Equifax has grown into the biggest credit bureau in the world.

Since there had never been a credit bureau before 1898, the idea behind the business was revolutionary. Cator Woolford had run a grocery business up until that point. This business required him to collect sensitive information about his customers to ensure their credit was good.

Cator figured that other businesses would probably want to verify the credit of their customers too. So, he came up with the idea of selling his customers' credit profiles to other merchants. His original thought was that he'd make enough money doing this side business to cover his grocery business's expenses. But, to his surprise, the business of selling consumer information became more profitable than his grocery business.

Cator got in touch with his brother, Guy, who was an attorney. The two of them planned to drive this business to a higher level. They formed the Retail Credit Company in Atlanta, Georgia, in 1898. The company targeted local grocery stores throughout Atlanta as their primary customers.

In the 1900s, Retail Credit Company expanded its target audience to the insurance industry. Over the 20th century, they expanded their services even further to banks, credit card companies, car dealerships, colleges, and other financial institutions.

In the 1960s, Retail Credit Company was already the largest credit bureau in existence. They had about 300 active branches across the United

States. The type of information they collected from consumers had expanded as well. In addition to collecting their names, addresses, and employment information, they also collected information about people's childhoods and marital status.

Retail Credit Company started to put their consumer information onto computers to handle all this new information and their growing list of consumers on file. Not only did this make storing consumer data easier to do, but it also allowed Retail Credit Company to share the information more easily with other companies paying to receive it.

By 1971, Retail Credit Company captured the interest of the federal government. Too many people were complaining their personal information was being sold without their consent. In response, the United States Congress passed legislation called the Fair Credit Reporting Act. It was the very first law passed which regulated how credit bureaus could gather and sell consumer information.

Retail Credit Company had trouble obeying the new law during the first few years after it passed. This forced the government to pass more regulations and restrictions. For instance, credit bureau employees could no longer receive bonus payments for collecting negative information about consumers. It had been done a lot in the past, unfortunately.

By 1979, the Retail Credit Company's reputation was virtually destroyed. As the company attempted to change its ways and build a better reputation, its leaders thought it would be wise to change its name to Equifax. The name is short for "Equitable Factual Information."

Under a new brand name, Equifax took off in the 1980s. It was an active competition with Experian and Trans Union as they all purchased smaller credit agencies and acquired their consumer files. Equifax was the biggest of the three, as they aligned themselves with at least 65 credit bureaus to grow their database.

In 1999, Equifax started selling credit monitoring services to consumers for the first time. It was around the time when identity theft became more common in society. Credit monitoring services were marketed to consumers as a way for them to check their credit and ensure no one was using their information to take out loans.

Equifax now has more than 401 million credit records of consumers from all over the world. Their headquarters continues to be in Atlanta, but they have operations in 14 different nations.

Trans Union

In 1968, Union Tank Car Company created a holding company by the name of Trans Union. This was 70 years after Equifax was created. Trans Union was not originally a credit bureau until it acquired the Credit Bureau of Cook County in 1969, just one year after its formation. Ever since then, Trans Union has been an active participant in the credit industry.

Trans Union did not start as a recognized credit bureau, though. It gradually grew popular over

many years by purchasing credit bureaus in major cities across the country. The company believed that a national credit database would better serve creditors and consumers.

Credit companies used to be local companies in major cities. Their consumer records were nothing more than filing cards in a cabinet drawer. But after Trans Union acquired the Credit Bureau of Cook County and several other city credit bureaus, they transferred the data on those file cards to their national database.

In 2002, Trans Union bought True Credit. It allowed them to sell credit information directly to consumers for the first time. Ever since then, their business became even more successful. They have more than 249 offices across the United States and other offices in 25 nations in the world.

Experian

In 1968, a major automotive electronics company named TRW Inc. had purchased another business called Credit Data. Quickly following the acquisition, TRW formed a subsidiary named TRW Information Systems and Services Inc. It would be the original name of their future company, Experian.

TRW Inc. had been around since 1901, under the name Cleveland Cap Screw Company. It manufactured screws and bolts for automobiles and airplanes. As it started manufacturing additional parts and accessories, it became a massive company in the United States.

By the 1960s, the company started selling more than automotive and electronic parts. They were now gathering and selling consumer data too. It was what eventually lead to the formation of TRW Information Systems in 1968. They collected credit information from their own customers as well as information from Credit Data.

Over the next 20 years, TRW Information Systems had millions of consumer data files on record. In 1986, TRW became the first credit agency to sell consumer data to consumers directly. They were way ahead of the other credit agencies in this endeavor.

Unfortunately, TRW experienced a series of setbacks in 1991. Thousands of consumers found that their credit reports had several inaccuracies and incorrect information on them, mostly concerning tax liens that were not real. The cases were resolved over time after several consumers sued TRW. The company settled all the cases without going to a civil trial.

TRW was determined to stay in the credit business and get things managed better. They developed a new database called CRIS (Constituent Relations Information Systems). Without any more errors or issues, TRW was valuable once again. In 1996, private investors paid more than $1 billion to purchase ownership of TRW. After that, the investors purchased the biggest credit agency in the United Kingdom too.

Once all the credit files from both agencies were merged, TRW changed its name to Experian. It has continued to have that name over the last 24 years now. During this time, Experian has expanded its credit monitoring services to consumers in more than 65 nations globally.

Innovis

In 1970, Associated Credit Bureaus was formed. It went through a series of name changes over the next two decades after various organizations purchased it. It was renamed to Consumers Credit Associates in 1989 and then renamed again to Innovis in 1997. It has kept that name ever since.

Despite Innovis not being considered one of the three main credit bureaus, it made history the first credit reporting agency to capture consumer data and store it into databases automatically. But compared to the other credit bureaus, Innovis is still a relatively new credit reporting agency.

After all, Equifax has been collecting consumer information and selling it for over 100 years. Equifax, Trans Union, and Experian all have hundreds of millions of consumer credit files on record. Most lenders and financial companies are not required to report credit information to Innovis.

In 2001, however, there was a breakthrough for the company after Freddie Mac and Fannie Mae required mortgage companies to start reporting credit information to Innovis. Still, it remains in the shadows of the other three credit agencies.

The Value of Bad Credit

Credit bureaus are businesses that need to make a profit. Their business model is to gather consumer credit data and then sell it to creditors as credit reports and leads. Creditors use this information to pressure consumers to apply for a new loan or increase the credit limit on their existing loan or credit card.

Have you ever received letters in the mail from lenders like Chase, where they try to convince you to sign up for a new credit card? Why do you think they keep sending you these letters? It is because they bought your consumer credit information from the primary credit bureaus and see that you have good credit (at least a score of 550).

The credit bureaus profit from selling this information to companies like Chase. These lenders will then turn around and try to persuade you to take out a new credit card that you don't necessarily need or want. But what may surprise you is that lenders pay more money to credit bureaus for consumers' credit information with sub-prime credit.

Sub-prime credit is very poor credit between a 300 and 579 credit score. When consumers have credit scores within this range, they are typically more than 30 days late on their loan or credit card payments. Lenders and creditors are willing to pay a lot of money for lists of consumers with sub-prime credit because they are the riskiest borrowers.

There are two possible reasons why a lender or creditor might have an interest in knowing which consumers are risky. One reason is they could flag these consumers immediately if one ever attempts to apply for a loan. But if the lender is a sub-prime credit card company or debt consolidation company, they might want to find people under financial strain and offer their services to them.

For instance, a debt consolidation company will issue a loan to consumers who pay off all their outstanding credit accounts. That means the consumer only has to make one monthly payment to one creditor instead of multiple payments to multiple creditors. If a debt consolidation company can find which consumers have multiple outstanding credit accounts, it could mean a lot of business for that company.

Creditors pay for lists of consumers with late credit card payments, high balances on credit cards, pre-foreclosures, foreclosures, bankruptcies, collections, late mortgage payments, and so on. Each of these situations creates lousy credit, which allows certain lenders to offer their debt relief services.

Again, it's all about the money. Lenders make more money by offering loan services to financially strapped people because they'll end up paying more interest on their debt consolidation loans, bankruptcy loans, or whatever other debt relief loans they get offered. Why would a lender waste their time offering loans to people with excellent credit?

Those people usually pay off their loans early, which means they don't pay much interest to the lenders. The lenders can only make money if borrowers pay more money in interest. So, it makes sense for the lenders to seek out people with bad credit because they'll stay obligated to a loan for a lot longer.

As for the credit bureaus, they're making even more money by selling this "bad credit" consumer information to all these companies. It also explains why credit bureaus don't care so much about accurate credit reports. The only reason they allow consumers to dispute information in their credit reports is that they're legally required to offer that option. Most consumers do not even do that because they don't check their credit reports too often.

The moral here is that credit bureaus do not care about consumers. They only care about making a profit with the companies willing to purchase the consumer information they've collected. It is up to you as a consumer to ensure your credit profile is accurate and in good standing.

What are Data Furnishers?

Data furnishers are for-profit loan companies who offer loans to consumers and report personal information, such as their payment history, to the three main credit bureaus. The data furnishers can be private or public companies.

Along with that payment history information, the reporting will also include the consumer's name, address, social security number, date of birth, current employer, previous addresses, and all previous credit inquiries from over the last ten years. The law requires data furnishers to report this information to the credit bureaus.

When data furnishers lend money, the consumers (borrowers) must pay a certain amount of interest each month. The consumer's level of risk determines the interest rate. Riskier consumers with low credit scores will pay a higher interest rate. And, of course, less risky consumers with high credit scores will pay a lower interest rate.

A credit card company will never charge 0% interest because they cannot make money that way. They depend on interest to sustain their profitability. That is why when a borrower makes a late payment, their interest rate goes up dramatically. Credit card companies tend to charge 13% to 28% interest when a borrower makes even one late payment.

Getting back to sub-prime consumers, they are three times more profitable to creditors because they tend to be late on their payments. In fact, creditors love late payments to a degree because it gives them the excuse to increase interest rates and charge late fees on top of them.

To make matters worse, creditors will increase your interest rates if your credit score decreases for some other reason. Creditors will recognize when your credit score goes down because they're always watching your credit report. Most consumers don't realize their credit reports are being observed by creditors so diligently.

Do not expect a phone call from your creditors to notify you of when your interest rates increase.

You'll just be surprised when you receive your next monthly bill in the mail. And if your credit report has errors, your creditors won't care to tell you about it unless it is terrible for them somehow. Otherwise, what's right for them is what's bad for you.

Request a Free Credit Report

It is your responsibility alone to ensure the accuracy of your credit profile. The credit bureaus and creditors will give you a hard time about it every step of the way. Sometimes the creditors won't notify the credit bureaus when your outstanding debts are paid. Either that or the credit bureaus won't notify the creditors when information in your credit report has been updated. It is up to you to notify them to ensure you're treated fairly.

The federal government grants consumers the right to request one free copy of their credit reports each year because they want to give consumers the chance to manage their credit profiles and ensure their accuracy. This law was passed due to the credit bureaus' reputation for not fixing inaccuracies themselves.

Since the federal government is not continually monitoring credit reports for inaccuracies, the consumers must do that for themselves. So, it is worth your time to request your free credit report and review it for mistakes.

Chapter 3 – How Credit Scores Work

Hopefully, you have requested your free credit report or at least have a good idea of what is in it, especially your credit score. It is so much easier to request a free credit report in this day and age because you can go online and request one at any time. Just go to AnnualCreditReport.com and request your free yearly credit report from all three credit bureaus.

It is imperative to learn your credit score and how it gets calculated in the first place. You'll then know how to make the necessary changes to increase your credit score and improve your credit report's standing.

Credit Score Models

The credit bureaus and credit reporting agencies use hundreds of credit scoring models to calculate consumers' credit scores. Fair Isaac is a company that has developed the most popular models. They use risk statistics to come up with a specific credit score number. These risk statistics score the likelihood of a consumer being over 90 days late with their debt payments over the next 24 months. If you're likely to be over 90 days late, you'll be given a low credit score.

Fair Isaac creates new scoring models all the time. The three credit bureaus are their biggest customers because they purchase these scoring models to use in the consumer credit reports they create for their own customers. Companies from various industries also purchase Fair Isaac's scoring models, including credit card companies, real estate companies, and banking companies.

Fair Isaac has hundreds of different scoring models available for different industries. The specific models for each industry can calculate a more accurate credit score to weigh the risk of issuing a particular loan, such as a car loan or home loan. Let's look at the auto industry's scoring models as an example.

When someone defaults on their car loan payments and their car gets repossessed, the person will have a lower "auto industry" credit score than the three credit bureaus' consumer credit score. Similarly, if someone misses a few credit card payments, it reflects worse on their credit card industry's credit score than their consumer credit score.

What you have here are different variables to the credit scores of different industries. A car loan company cares more about your auto history than they do about your credit card history. Similarly, a credit card company cares more about your credit card history than your auto history.

Credit Scorecards

Credit scorecards is a fancy way of referring to credit variables. Even though hundreds of different credit models exist, they contain many of the same mechanisms for calculating a credit score.

However, the variables of some models have more of an effect on credit scores than other variables. But overall, a credit score is usually calculated based on the history of payments, amount of credit spent, duration of credit history, the amount of new debt, and the number of credit accounts.

History of Payments

Approximately 35% of your credit score is based on your history of making monthly payments toward your debts. It considers all the payments you made to lenders and creditors, and particularly when you made them. All negative information related to your payments, such as late payments or defaulted accounts, will significantly decrease your credit score.

Late payments will affect your credit score very quickly because creditors usually report to credit bureaus every month. That means if you missed last month's mortgage payment, for example, then your credit score will decrease over the current month.

Under the mortgage industry scoring model, your credit score could decrease by more than 120 points if you were late for one month. You lose so many points because the scoring model believes you are at a greater risk of missing more payments and could likely default on your mortgage.

One thing should be emphasized, though. Creditors will not report a late payment to the credit bureaus until it is 30 days late. With that being said, it takes creditors about ten days to process payments in their system. So, if you send your late payment 25 days after it was due, then you could still see a negative rating on your credit report.

Making your payments on time is the best thing you can do to keep a high credit score. The 35% difference it makes goes a long way in sustaining the strength of your credit report.

Amount of Credit Spent

Approximately 30% of your credit score is based on the amount of credit you've spent than your credit limits. For instance, if your credit card account has an $8,000 limit and you've spent $7,000 of it while making the minimum monthly payments, then your credit score will decrease. It is always better to pay off most of your credit card balance as early as possible. That will keep your credit score high.

One trick to increase your credit score is to apply for a credit card with a high credit limit but then spend very little credit on it. If you have a more significant gap between the amount you've spent on the card and its credit limit, then it will improve your credit score tremendously.

But remember this 30% variable factors in all of your credit accounts. For instance, if you have an outstanding car loan or mortgage loan, it will lower your credit score in the beginning because you will owe a lot more money to creditors. But as you keep making payments on the loan and reduce the balance owed, it will gradually increase your credit score over time.

Credit cards are different because you don't initially owe your credit limit if you haven't maxed out your credit card. You only start owing money after you make purchases with the card. If you only spend 10%

of your credit limit and then pay it back every month or so, then your credit score will stay high. That is the difference between how a credit card affects your credit score versus a car loan or home loan.

A lot of financially responsible people make the mistake of paying off their installment loans too early. In their minds, they assume it is a good thing to decrease their debt by making more significant monthly payments than what is owed each month. The problem is that if you pay off your loans early, you won't build much of a payment history. That goes back to the previous factor.

What you need to remember is not to overextend yourself with debt. Take out loans only if you need them. Make your monthly payments on the loans on-time without paying them off too quickly. But it is okay to make bigger payments to reduce the balance owed on them when it comes to credit cards.

Duration of Credit History

Approximately 15% of your credit score revolves around the duration of your credit history. Do not confuse this with the history of your debt payments because they're two different things. Credit history simply means how long you've had credit in general.

When you turn 18 years old and get a car loan or credit card for the first time, your credit score will not be anywhere near 800 because you have no credit history. It takes many years of establishing a credit history before you can reach toward a credit score of 800 (assuming you've satisfied the other factors).

The biggest challenge for a young person is to get approved for a loan without a credit history. It forces them to ask someone else with a credit history, such as their mother or father, to co-sign the loan for them. A co-signer is someone who agrees to be financially responsible for the borrower's debt in case they default on the loan. You can use their credit history as a way to get approval for a loan. Then you can build your credit history with it.

Another way for a young person to build their credit history is to get added as an authorized user on a family member's credit card account. Some scoring models do not award points for this, though, so be careful with that. But it is an excellent way to score points on some models, especially if you have not gotten a car loan yet.

Amount of New Debt

Approximately 10% of your credit score is based on how much new debt you carry. If you currently have several outstanding credit accounts and attempt to apply for more loans or credit card accounts, it will hurt your credit score.

The credit models look at the number of credit accounts, how long they've been open, and how many times you've applied for new credit over the last 12 months. In fact, each time you apply for credit, it lowers your credit score.

Whenever creditors request your credit report from the three credit bureaus, it is considered a credit inquiry. If you have too many credit inquiries, it lowers your credit score because it means you're trying to apply for too many loans or credit cards within a short period. That is never a good thing, even if they're credit cards

The rule of thumb is that you should never apply for more than one loan or credit card within one month. If you can wait six months to a year, it is even better.

Number of Credit Accounts

Approximately 10% of your credit score is based on how many credit accounts you have open. If you have more variety in your accounts, it will positively impact your credit score.

For instance, it is better to have a mortgage loan, car loan, and two credit cards than it is to have only three credit cards with no other credit accounts. Multiple credit cards are always a bad thing for your credit report. Just like it is terrible if you have multiple car loans or multiple mortgages. Credit models prefer a healthy mixture of credit accounts.

But here is the exciting thing. Credit models tend to favor consumers with three credit cards than those with less or more than three. You still need other credit accounts too, such as a mortgage or car loan, but three credit cards usually will give you the highest credit score.

Final Thoughts

Don't believe the sentiment that you must cancel your credit cards to improve your credit and get out of debt. If you have three credit card accounts with high credit limits, you can improve your credit as long as you don't charge too much on them.

Creditors use all kinds of scoring models, so there is never a way to know for sure. But the factors we just mentioned are your best bet in boosting your credit score and keeping it high.

Chapter 4 – How to Understand Your Credit Report

You'll see a lot of companies on the internet trying to sell you access to your credit report. They might even attempt to advertise something like "Get a Free Credit Report," as if you didn't know that you're entitled to one by law.

Then as you sign up for an account to get your free credit report, the company will ask you for a credit card number. The fine print might even tell you that you're going to be charged a monthly fee after 30 days for their credit monitoring service.

If you're worried about identity theft or someone using your financial information without your knowledge, then you might find a credit monitoring service to be a worthy investment. The system will alert you whenever there is new activity on your credit report. You can also update your credit report every 30 days to see if new information is on it, including a new credit score.

A lot of people don't feel comfortable giving their credit card information online. Either that or they don't want to pay $30 per month for a credit monitoring service they won't use too often. It all depends on your level of concern over your finances and identity.

If you'd prefer a quick and easy way to get your free credit report without a hidden agenda, it is best to visit www.annualcreditreport.com. It is a government-run website that gives you a simple way to get your credit report for free. No catches.

Alternatively, you can call toll-free at 1-877-322-8228 to receive your credit report via the telephone. But if you'd rather have the written version, you can visit www.ftc.gov/credit and download a credit report request form. Print out the form, fill it out and mail it to:

Credit Report Request Service
PO BOX 105281
Atlanta, GA 30348-5281

A mail request will take the longest to fulfill. It could take as long as 15 days after mailing the request before receiving your report in the mail.

How to Read Your Credit Report

If you have obtained a free copy of your credit report, you've accomplished the first step. Now you have the task of reading through all the information on the report and understanding what it means exactly.

If you can learn how to interpret the data correctly, you'll know how to spot mistakes and errors in the reporting. As you spot mistakes in the report, highlight each one so you'll know to dispute it later.

Personal Profile

The first section of your credit report is the personal profile. It contains your name, current address, previous addresses, current employer, previous employers, aliases (AKA), and birth date.

Check this information to see if it is accurate. Something as simple as a spelling error should be disputed.

Focus on the aliases in particular. They are the different names entered into the computer at various times when you've applied for loans or credit cards. Suppose you apply for a car loan, and the salesperson misspells your name when they pull your credit report.

Since the name they entered is linked to your social security number, it will be submitted to the three credit bureaus and placed as an alias on your credit report. If you don't want that alias on your report, you must dispute it and request it to be removed.

Now do the same thing with your address information. If you see an address misspelled or an address you never lived before, request to have the address removed through a dispute. Go on to do the same thing with your employment information and date of birth.

All the information must be 100% accurate and valid. That way, your credit profile does not get confused with other similar credit profiles in the system. Believe it or not, these mix-ups happen quite frequently.

Credit Inquiries

Each time you apply for a loan or credit card, a credit inquiry is listed on your credit report. If you have too many inquiries within a short timeframe, it indicates that your spending habits might be a bit extreme to future creditors. It also lowers your credit score and makes you a high-risk applicant.

If you apply for a loan and the application gets denied, the denial will be listed on your credit report. Don't fall into the trap of applying for loans at different lending institutions because it will keep dragging down your credit score each time you get denied. Then you'll have even less of a chance to get approved. Not only that, but employers might look down upon those credit inquiries when you go to apply for jobs.

Approximately 10% of your credit score gets affected each time you apply for new credit. Too many inquiries within a short time will decrease your credit score. That is why if you get denied credit one time, you should request a copy of your credit report to see if any errors are on it. Those errors could be what is causing you to get denied in the first place. Then you can dispute the errors and fix your credit report before applying for another loan.

Account Summary

The account summary section gives you an overview of all the information on your credit report. You'll see information about the number of active accounts open, number of accounts closed, real estate accounts, credit card accounts, debt in collections, outstanding debt, and so on.

Study the information in the summary section carefully. Check the accuracy of the balances and the accounts that are listed as active and closed. Make sure you check the accuracy of your three credit reports from the three credit bureaus. Each credit bureau has its own separate credit report on you. Sometimes the information on one report will have some differences compared to the information on another report. If you see differences that should not be there, you need to dispute them.

The differences are not always minor. If one credit bureau has not received updated information for your credit report, it will have outdated or incomplete information. You must check everything for accuracy, such as the accounts open, accounts closed, balances, debts owed, number of inquiries, collection accounts, and so on.

Pay particular attention to the derogatory section involving delinquencies because any inaccurate information in this section could be what's dragging down your credit score. Dispute all inaccurate information that you find to correct it.

Account History

Most credit reports create categories for different credit accounts in the account history section. You could have categories for revolving accounts, real estate accounts, public records, installment loans, and so on.

Every account listed in each section will indicate the creditor's name, the date the account opened, account number, high balance, amount of the monthly payment, the balance owed, and past due amount. The account status of each account will show as an unpaid collection, open, or closed account.

It is quite common for inaccuracies to be present. Each inaccuracy will severely affect your credit score, so dispute them when they're discovered. The Payment Status section is where it counts the most. You'll see payment history from over the last 24 months. The payments on an account will be listed as Paid, Collection, 30 Days Late, 60 Days Late, 90 Days Late, or 120 Days Late.

Look at the items listed as late. Sometimes you might submit a payment to a creditor, but they never reported it to the credit bureaus. That will cause it to be listed as late because the bureaus haven't gotten the updated information. It is your job to dispute the information and request the proper updates to be applied.

Public Records

Public records include things like tax liens, judgments, and bankruptcies. It is better to have no public records because only derogatory things show up in public records. So, if you see anything listed in your public records section, pay close attention to it. Each public record item will indicate the record type, account number, court docket, date filed, and other crucial information like that.

Bankruptcy accounts stay on your credit report for ten years. Court judgments could stay on your credit report for over ten years. Tax liens could stay on your report for any number of years. For this reason, the public records section is the most severe section of your credit report. You must do everything possible to avoid getting items listed in this section.

That means avoiding bankruptcies, lawsuits, and foreclosures.

Everything Else

As you can see from reading this chapter, it is beneficial to your financial health that you request a free credit report. Then you can make sure it is accurate with the latest information about your credit. Whenever you spot an inaccuracy, dispute it with the appropriate credit bureau to have it removed and replaced. Then you can ensure that you have the highest credit score possible.

Chapter 5 – The Credit Repair Process

Credit repair is a process where the consumer disputes inaccuracies, errors, and questionable data on their credit reports. These are usually negative markings or items on their reports that drive down their credit score. Naturally, the consumer wants to dispute these items and have them removed to increase their credit score.

In 1971, the U.S. Congress passed the Fair Credit Reporting Act and it was signed into law. It granted consumers the right to dispute errors, unverifiable information, and other inaccuracies in their credit reports. There have been several amendments to the law in the decades since it was first passed, but the law's primary function has remained the same.

In 2003, the Fair and Accurate Credit Transaction Act (FACTA) allowed new sections to be added to the original law. Not only did FACTA expand coverage for consumers, but it gave them the legal right to receive one free copy of their credit report from each of the three credit bureaus per year. It also regulated creditors' actions a lot more, mainly how they handle identity theft cases and send out fraud alerts to consumers.

Best of all, creditors are required to respond to disputes in a timely fashion and determine whether they're valid or not.

Is Credit Repair Effective?

There is a lot of skepticism about whether credit repair is genuinely effective. Creditors and credit bureaus go out of their way to convince consumers that credit repair is a myth and that nothing can be done to fix bad credit.

Why do they say this? It goes back to what we talked about before. Creditors and credit bureaus profit from selling consumer information, especially negative consumer information. They don't want consumers disputing and repairing their credit reports because it means their information won't be as valuable to sell to other creditors.

Therefore, you can rest assured that credit repair is real and very effective at boosting your credit score. The level of effectiveness depends on how you dispute the inaccuracies in your report. For instance, you must understand their E-Oscar and OCR computer systems before you file a dispute with the credit bureaus, whether it's by mail or online.

Most people assume filing a dispute is as simple as filling out a form and sending it to the credit bureaus. But it is a little more complicated than that. You have to file the correct way, or else your dispute might not be taken seriously.

How to Repair Credit Effectively

Before the internet, consumers had to mail letters to the credit bureaus to dispute information in their credit reports. Once the disputes were entered into the system, the creditors had 30 days to respond, or else the disputed items were removed from the reports. In many instances, the items were removed after 30 days because the mail system was slower and more confusing for managing disputes.

Now that has all changed. Disputes and responses to disputes are made electronically. Creditors still have 30 days to respond, but the window is wider because they don't have to wait for the mail system to deliver the disputes to them. However, the deleted items can technically be put back on the report after 30 days if the creditors respond late or make a mistake.

It is up to you as the consumer to check your credit report and ensure the negative items are removed permanently. Fortunately, the three credit bureaus have established two automated computer systems that allow the dispute process to move along smoothly.

Let's examine those two systems below.

OCR

OCR means "Optical Character Recognition." Credit bureaus use this computer technology to automatically analyze dispute letters and determine if the arguments in them are legitimate or not. If the system believes the consumer is attempting to improve their credit score without making a legitimate claim, your dispute will be flagged and stalled.

Disputes are automatically categorized based on their level of legitimacy. A reason code for the dispute is generated as well. That means if you try to dispute the same problem in the future, it will get rejected automatically.

Credit bureaus want to reduce their workload, so they depend on OCR technology to reduce human error while eliminating as many illegitimate disputes as possible. The computer system scans every dispute letter variable, including the spelling, font colors, type of paper, font type, and more.

A lot of people use template letters to file similar disputes repeatedly. The OCR technology checks every variable to see if they're similar to previous disputes you filed. If this is detected, the system will mark your dispute as frivolous. From there, your dispute will be disregarded without any human-led investigation whatsoever.

For this reason, we do not recommend filing an online dispute. Computer systems process online disputes, which means they could be marked as frivolous even when legitimate. Credit bureaus encourage online disputes to reduce the chance of any changes being made to them.

Confuse the System

Okay, so how do you get your dispute past the automated OCR scanning process? Basically, you'll want your dispute letter to confuse the system into not knowing whether it's legitimate or frivolous. You do this by creating a dispute letter, which looks like no other letter. That is why you never use templates to write your dispute letters.

When you write a dispute letter, your goal must be to get it presented to a human. For example, if you intentionally misspell words and use magic markers to write your dispute letter, it would confuse the OCR computer system. Then you increase the likelihood of the system sending the dispute letter to a human for review.

Another tactic is to write your dispute on a piece of heavy stock paper or card stock. Thick paper like this cannot be processed through the OCR system, which is a sure way of getting it processed by a human instead.

Next, use unusual fonts and colors to write your dispute letter. Misspell the occasional word in each paragraph. It might seem like an unprofessional thing to do, but that's the point. You don't want your dispute letter to look like a professional credit repair company wrote it. That is how you confuse the OCR system.

And, of course, handwrite your dispute letter rather than type it. Handwriting is unique to every individual, making your letter look more original and genuine for sure. Choose a pen, pencil, marker, or crayon to do the handwriting.

If you follow these steps, you will have a better chance of getting your dispute letters approved.

e-OSCAR

e-OSCAR stands for "Online Solution for Complete and Accurate Reporting." The three primary credit bureaus use the e-OSCAR system to automate the dispute process. It inputs the disputes into the computer and then sends the disputes to the actual creditors or data furnishers associated with them.

e-OSCAR has a better track record of eliminating human error. It analyzes your dispute and generates a two-digit reason code for it automatically. The reason code represents why the dispute was filed. For instance, claiming you were not late on a payment would have one code. Claiming an outstanding credit account is fully paid would be another code.

When creditors receive your dispute, they will immediately look at the reason code to recognize why the dispute was filed. It saves them time from having to read through each dispute letter to get the reason. Many people tend to write long drawn out stories about their financial situation when they write their disputes. Creditors don't have time to read these stories, which is why they focus specifically on the reason code.

Once the creditor knows the two-character reason code, the account in dispute, and the name on the account, they will validate or invalidate the dispute. If the creditor fails to respond within 30 days, the disputed item will be removed. The creditor only has to click one button to validate the dispute and remove the disputed item.

However, there have been disputes over whether real investigations occur when the e-OSCAR system is used. Many claims indicate that creditors click validate or invalidate without conducting a thorough investigation into the dispute first.

Again, Confuse the System

You cannot trust any computer system to do the right thing. Even though the e-OSCAR system has a better performance rate, you'll still want your dispute letter to look original. Use the same tips mentioned for the OCR to ensure a human will investigate your dispute letter.

Chapter 6 – Inaccurate Account Disputes

Nearly three-fourths of all credit reports contain at least one error or inaccuracy in them. Consumers are doing an injustice to themselves if they don't review their credit reports at least once per year. The slightest inaccuracy could make a significant difference in restoring a credit report to a satisfactory level.

There is no such thing as a reasonable mistake on a credit report. It is even worse if you have negative credit accounts listed that have already been paid and settled. If you review your credit report and find a negative account that should be removed, then you must dispute the account on the report to remove it.

Common mistakes might include the wrong date of default on your loan payments or duplicate accounts with slightly different account numbers. You might even see the wrong balanced owed on a credit account by thousands of dollars. If the creditor did not update the credit bureaus about the account status, then the last reported balance will remain on the credit report.

Do not assume simple things like date of default errors are minor and insignificant. They can have a long-lasting impact on your credit score if you don't dispute them and get them fixed. Plus, such a date can determine how long the creditor has to pursue legal action against you to reclaim the money you owe them. If the statute of limitations expires before they pursue legal action, then you are protected under the law.

Duplicate credit accounts would be severely damaging because it would indicate you have double the debt than you actually do. No one should have to be responsible for more debt than they owe. Dispute any duplicate account so that you can increase your credit score to its proper position.

You are the only beneficiary of a healthy and accurate credit profile. Please exercise your right to request a free credit report and review it thoroughly. Every single minor error or inaccuracy should be disputed for the sake of your credit profile and financial standing. It could mean the difference in whether you get approved for a loan or job.

Do you know why the Fair Credit Reporting Act was passed into law in the first place? It is because the credit bureaus were so dishonest with consumers about their information. The bureaus would also sell their data to other creditors without their consent. Since the legislation was passed, many consumers have sued credit bureaus for continuing to misuse their information.

With that being said, there is no outside force that watches your credit report and notifies you when errors are on it. The Fair Credit Reporting Act calls for consumers to file disputes on their behalf if they see errors in their credit reports. Disputing a credit report comes in the form of sending a dispute letter to the three credit bureaus. The letter must identify the inaccuracies and why you believe they should be removed from your credit reports.

You'll find dispute letter examples near the end of the chapter. Each letter represents a different scenario where you would need to dispute something in your credit report. Use the letters as examples to work from when you write your dispute letters.

Don't just copy the letters word for word because the computer system might flag your dispute letter as frivolous. You learned about that in the previous chapter.

Dispute Codes

As was previously discussed, the e-OSCAR computer system assigns a two-digit reason code to explain why a dispute was filed and the claim being made in it. These codes will quickly tell the computer system whether a dispute letter is likely frivolous or not.

FACTA gives credit bureaus the right to ignore disputes that are deemed frivolous. If you dispute the same credit account over the same complaint, then it gets labeled frivolous. Sending multiple disputes over the same complaint will not make the inaccuracy go away any faster.

Credit bureaus are very sensitive about their time. They don't want to waste time by reviewing the same disputes repeatedly. That is why they put computer systems in place to detect similar disputes and to mark them frivolous automatically. So, send one dispute at a time and list all the inaccuracies you find in it. Wait until that dispute is settled before you send another dispute.

The credit bureaus use 27 different reason codes for dispute letters sent to them. Each code is two characters long and represents a particular reason for the dispute. The e-OSCAR system is responsible for setting the reason code automatically. If you followed the advice above, your dispute letter should not get labeled frivolous by the system. Instead, it will be sent to a human for review.

How Many Items to Dispute?

There is confusion amongst consumers regarding how many items to dispute at once on their credit reports. According to research, it makes no difference whether you dispute one account or all accounts if you discover inaccurate or unverifiable data on them.

The OCR system is responsible for entering the dispute information into the e-OSCAR computer system. If you send too many dispute letters at once, then it might cause the system to send the letters over to a human for review. That is okay because at least the disputed information will quickly get entered into the system, which means it will reach the creditors a lot sooner.

Each account complaint is a separate dispute letter. A human investigator or their OCR computer system will review these letters for sure. Nothing will stop them from being investigated. After the e-OSCAR system receives the letter's dispute information, each creditor is sent only the information related to your disputed account with them. They won't get to see all the accounts you're disputing at the same time. Each creditor only sees the disputed accounts over which they have control over.

We recommend you send one dispute letter with all of the inaccuracies listed on them. Even though it is possible to simultaneously send multiple dispute letters, you don't want to risk any of them getting flagged for their similarities. You're better off using one letter with multiple disputes on it.

Besides, the computer system will process the disputes much faster if there is one letter. Otherwise, each dispute letter will get processed one at a time, so you will have to wait longer for results.

How to Write a Dispute Letter

You must put all the right content in your dispute letter without missing anything. If certain information is missing from the letter, it could delay or prevent your dispute letter from getting processed.

The basic information to enter includes your first name, last name, home address, and social security number. Make sure you write down all this information accurately. The credit bureaus will verify this information to ensure the right person is filing the dispute. The social security number is the most crucial piece of information to get right. It is what connects you directly to your credit profile with the three credit bureaus. More importantly, it is how the credit bureaus verify your identity.

However, they will need more information than just your social security number to verify your identity. They will also need copies of your social security card and photo identification. No investigations of your disputes will take place until you provide this documentation.

A driver's license is the most common form of photo identification. If you don't have that or another state-approved photo ID card, you can produce your U.S. passport as an acceptable photo ID. If you don't have your social security card, then you can provide your W2 tax form or pay-stub that has your social security number on it.

If you dispute a particular account, then include the account number and account name on your dispute letter. Be sure to write the name of the creditor as well. This will make it easier for the credit bureau to locate the creditor and provide them with your dispute information.

If one dispute letter is disputing multiple credit accounts, provide the necessary information for each account on the letter.

Choosing a Dispute Letter

You must use a unique dispute letter for each specific reason for why you're filing the dispute. If you have multiple reasons, then sending multiple dispute letters might be more justified. For instance, if you're disputing a late payment and an account that is not yours, then send a separate dispute letter for each one. That might work out better.

If the creditor reviews your dispute letter and does not verify the problem you specified, then you cannot send another dispute letter for that same reason. But what you can do is send another dispute letter about the same account for a different reason. If your account is no longer on file with the creditor, they probably won't respond to you at all. They will also request for the credit bureaus to delete the account from the credit report.

If you are confident the disputed account is invalid or closed, you must provide documentation to prove it to the credit bureaus. Otherwise, they won't take your case seriously and will disregard it from this point forward. But keep in mind that the creditors won't see the dispute letters and documentation you send to the credit bureaus.

For this reason, we recommend you send separate dispute letters to the creditors. They might go ahead and notify the credit bureaus on your behalf if they can verify your dispute is valid. We'll supply you with sample dispute letters that can be sent to both credit bureaus and creditors.

Sometimes you might dispute an account, but only to have the credit bureaus come back and say it is a valid account. When this kind of thing happens, do not give up if you believe it is truly invalid. File another dispute for a DIFFERENT REASON but related to the account in question. If the credit bureaus end up agreeing with your reason, they will delete the necessary items from the account as needed.

Prepare to Mail Your Dispute Letter

Keep a list of the negative items you found in your credit report. You'll want to track those items later after you send your dispute letter and get it reviewed.

But first, you should choose the right dispute letter based on the nature of your reason, such as an unverifiable account or an error or inaccuracy in the account. Once you find the right letter, fill in the necessary information discovered in this chapter previously. When you're done writing the letter, sign it on the bottom to make it official.

Double-check the letter's information for accuracy, such as the creditors' names, your social security number, and all of the relevant account numbers associated with your dispute. If you don't have the right account numbers listed, the credit bureaus cannot verify your claim.

Each credit bureau works independently from one another. You cannot mail one dispute letter to one bureau and expect all three bureaus to resolve your problem. After all, the credit report from one credit bureau might not have the same errors as it does on the credit report from another credit bureau. Therefore, you have to send a separate dispute letter to each credit bureau, and it must indicate the unique errors on the credit report it has on file for you. Again, we recommend mailing the letters through the post office to the credit bureaus rather than emailing them online. Record the date on which the disputes were mailed. Each credit bureau might have more than one address listed. Always go with the first address listed.

After you've mailed your dispute letters to the credit bureaus, you'll have to wait anywhere from 30 to 45 days for a response. Sometimes it takes as long as 40 to 45 days, depending on how busy they are. Once they do respond, they'll let you know the results of their investigations.

When the credit bureaus receive the dispute letters and enter the information into their e-OSCAR computer systems, the creditors have 30 days from the latter date to respond to the disputes. The reason you might have to wait up to 45 days is that the credit bureaus will need time to receive your letters and input them into their e-OSCAR systems. That will probably take 7 to 14 days alone. After that, the creditors have 30 days to receive the dispute information and respond to it.

FACTA is the legislation that enforces these time limits, such as the 30 days for the creditors to respond. FACTA also requires credit bureaus to mail you the dispute results if you made this request in writing on your dispute letters. If so, the law requires them to obey your request and mail you the results. Along with the results, the bureaus are required to include copies of your credit reports. The reports will arrive in large envelopes and have P.O. Boxes listed on the return labels.

Remember that you'll receive three separate credit reports in the mail from the three credit bureaus. The dispute results should be on the first page of your credit reports. The appearance of the reports might look slightly different from one another. That is normal.

Reading the Results

Here is how to read the results from each credit bureau:

Trans Union

When you receive your Trans Union reports in the mail, they are straightforward to understand. The results' first page has all the information listed clearly, such as your account number, account name, and the dispute results. Some of the terms you might see for the results include Deleted, Verified, New Information Below, or No Change.

Suppose you have new information on the report. In that case, it could mean the negative item was only modified, or a simple little correction was made to what you disputed initially, such as a date and balance amount owed. Also, your Trans Union account details will be provided to you. They will let you log into your online Trans Union account and see an updated copy of your credit report online.

Experian

Experian will give you the results on the first or second page of your report. They will even provide a list summary that highlights the crucial details of the results. It will contain the account name, status, and number.

The account status will be "Reviewed," "Updated," "Deleted," or "Remains." The status you want to see is "Deleted" because it means the disputed account was deleted. If you see "Remains" as the status, it means the disputed account was not changed and will remain on your credit report.

"Updated" means a minor error in your report was fixed, such as a spelling mistake or inaccurate account number. "Reviewed" status could mean an update or deletion was made, but you have to find it yourself in the credit report. It is unusual to see "Reviewed" status, though.

You can expect to see standard details about the account in question as well. Some of these details include the name, address, and phone number of the creditor overseeing the account.

Equifax

It is a bit more challenging to understand the results of the Equifax reports. They don't summarize the results in any particular section, so you have to review your report to find the changes yourself. If any of the accounts were deleted or updated, you should see them listed on the first or second pages. Look for a category title like "Collection Agency" or "The Results of Our Investigation."

When you find the results information, you'll see the creditor's name and the number of the disputed account. Then it should give you a one-sentence explanation of the results. Look for the words "DELETE," "UPDATE," or "VERIFY" to indicate that changes were made to your Equifax credit report.

Whenever an update is applied, Equifax will give you more information in the summary description section.

Last Payment Date

Review the three credit reports to see what was changed and not changed. Use a highlighter to mark the negative accounts that remain on the report. You can file a separate dispute for each negative account on it.

Credit reports give you more details compared to credit monitoring reports. For instance, Experian will give you "Last Reported," Trans Union will give you "Date Paid," and Equifax will give "Date of 1st Delinquency." These dates are important because they indicate when the last payment was made on the account.

When you stop making payments on a credit account, it becomes a derogatory account on your credit report. This negative indicator will remain on your credit report for seven years, starting from the date of your last payment. That is why you'll want to make a note of that date.

Repeat These Steps

Have you kept track of all the negative items on your credit reports? You must do this whenever you request your credit report from each of the three credit bureaus.

As your credit reports become updated from various disputes, you'll see more and more negative marks removed from your future credit reports. It indicates that more of your creditors now have accurate information about your history.

Creditors are not good at keeping accurate records, which forces consumers to have to file disputes frequently. Sometimes creditors will accidentally delete your account after they sell your consumer data to other companies. Then it will reflect on your credit report.

It places you in a position where you must keep disputing your reports to update the information. You won't likely clear up all the inaccuracies with one dispute letter to each credit bureau. It will be an ongoing process where you send one dispute letter to each bureau monthly. And in those letters, you indicate a new reason so that it is not labeled as frivolous by the computer system.

Don't forget that you'll be disputing your credit report with both the creditors and credit bureaus separately. Since creditors and credit bureaus don't always update each other, it is up to you to notify each one to ensure your records stay accurate on both sides.

Follow the same pattern each time the credit bureaus send your dispute results to you. Review the results, record the changes made, record the inaccuracies still present, and then write new dispute letters to the credit bureaus for different reasons than before.

If the credit bureaus don't send you back your credit reports, use their credit monitoring services to request your reports online. Sometimes the credit bureaus like to stall by not sending the reports to you. Once you've waited more than 40 days without getting the results in the mail, you need to request your reports online. Then you can see whether the credit bureaus did an investigation into your disputes.

It is possible the credit bureaus did an investigation and updated your credit reports but did not send the reports back to you in the mail. That is why having a credit monitoring service is crucial because you can receive updated information on your credit report immediately.

Chapter 7 – Sample Dispute Letters

We've written a lot about dispute letters in this book. Now you've come to the portion of the chapter that provides you with ten sample dispute letters. Each letter accommodates a specific reason for an account dispute on your credit report. Please choose the appropriate letter for your dispute reason and modify it accordingly. Try to make it read a little differently so that it doesn't get detected as frivolous by the e-OSCAR system.

First Sample Dispute Letter

Use the following sample dispute letter if you find a creditor listed on your credit report that you do not recognize.

Credit Bureau Name   Your Name
Credit Bureau Address   Your Address
Credit Bureau City, State, and Zip   Your City, State, Zip
                                                       Your Date of Birth
Date   Your Social Security Number

Dear CREDIT BUREAU NAME,
Re: Account Name and Number

I am contacting you regarding some information that I found to be inaccurate in my credit report.

I do not recognize this creditor on my report at all. I request that you verify the information and remove any inaccurate information from my credit report as quickly as possible. The items in question are:

CREDITOR'S NAME

ACCOUNT NUMBER

Once you're done, please provide me with an updated credit report reflecting the changes.

Thank you for your time,
YOUR SIGNATURE,
YOUR FIRST AND LAST NAME

Second Sample Dispute Letter

Use the following sample dispute letter if you are reporting outdated information on your credit report.

Credit Bureau Name   Your Name
Credit Bureau Address   Your Address
Credit Bureau City, State, and Zip   Your City, State, Zip
                                                                 Your Date of Birth
Date   Your Social Security Number

Dear CREDIT BUREAU NAME,
Re: Account Name and Number

After a review of my credit report, I discovered outdated information on it. I am writing to request the removal of this outdated information. Below are the outdated items I would like removed.

DETAILS OF OUTDATED ITEMS ON THE ACCOUNT GO HERE

In compliance with the Fair Credit Reporting Act, Section 605 [15 U.S.C. § 1681c] of *"Running of Reporting Period",* as of December 29th, 1997, reporting periods only run for 7 years or 10 years. It all depends on the type of information. In my case, the information in question expired as of [insert date].

I respectfully request an investigation of my claim. If you find it to be valid, then I would ask that you remove the outdated items immediately, as identified in this letter. If you discover any other outdated items over the course of your investigation, please remove them as well. After you have updated my credit report, I would request that you forward to me an updated copy of my credit report at the address listed above.

Finally, if your investigation finds the information to be accurate already, then I respectfully request that you forward to me a description of the procedure used to determine the accuracy and completeness of the item in question. In accordance with the FCRA I respectfully request you forward this information within 15 days of the completion of your re-investigation.

Thank you for your time and cooperation in resolving this matter. If you have any questions concerning this issue, I can be reached at: {insert daytime phone number including area code).

Sincerely,

Thank you for your time,
YOUR SIGNATURE
YOUR FIRST AND LAST NAME
YOUR SOCIAL SECURITY NUMBER

Third Sample Dispute Letter

Use the following sample dispute letter if you find incorrect account numbers on your credit report.

Credit Bureau Name   Your Name

Credit Bureau Address   Your Address

Credit Bureau City, State, and Zip   Your City, State, Zip

Your Date of Birth

Date   Your Social Security Number

Dear CREDIT BUREAU NAME,

Re: Account Name and Number

After a careful analysis of my credit report, I discovered some inaccurate information in it that I would like to bring to your attention.

The account number listed on my report doesn't match any of my records. I request that you verify the information and remove any inaccurate information from my credit report as quickly as possible. The items in question are:

CREDITOR'S NAME

ACCOUNT NUMBER

After doing so please provide me with an updated credit report reflecting the changes.

Thank you for your time,

YOUR SIGNATURE

YOUR FIRST AND LAST NAME

Fourth Sample Dispute Letter

Use the following sample dispute letter if your credit report lists an amount owed that is not correct.

Credit Bureau Name   Your Name

Credit Bureau Address   Your Address

Credit Bureau City, State, and Zip   Your City, State, Zip

                                                     Your Date of Birth

Date   Your Social Security Number

Dear CREDIT BUREAU NAME,

Re: Account Name and Number

I decided to contact you because I found some information that is inaccurate on my credit report.

The amount that is reported I owe is inaccurate as it is reported. I request that you verify the information and remove any inaccurate information from my credit report as quickly as possible. The items in question are:

CREDITOR'S NAME

ACCOUNT NUMBER

After doing so, please provide me with an updated credit report reflecting the changes.

Thank you for your time,
YOUR SIGNATURE
YOUR FIRST AND LAST NAME

Fifth Sample Dispute Letter

Use the following sample dispute letter if your credit report shows an incorrect balance on any of the accounts.

Credit Bureau Name	Your Name
Credit Bureau Address	Your Address
Credit Bureau City, State, and Zip	Your City, State, Zip
	Your Date of Birth
Date	Your Social Security Number

Dear CREDIT BUREAU NAME,

Re: Account Name and Number

I decided to contact you because I found some information that is inaccurate on my credit report.

The balance you are reporting I owe is incorrect, and doesn't match my records. I request that you verify the information and remove any inaccurate information from my credit report as quickly as possible. The items in question are:

CREDITOR'S NAME

ACCOUNT NUMBER

After doing so please provide me with an updated credit report reflecting the changes.

YOUR SIGNATURE
YOUR FIRST AND LAST NAME

Sixth Sample Dispute Letter

Use the following sample dispute letter for general disputes made on your credit report.

Credit Bureau Name   Your Name

Credit Bureau Address   Your Address

Credit Bureau City, State, and Zip   Your City, State, Zip

                                                      Your Date of Birth

Date   Your Social Security Number

Dear CREDIT BUREAU NAME,

Re: Account Name and Number

I am formally requesting for the inaccurate information in my credit report to be corrected. The item(s) that are listed below are incorrect and need to be deleted from my credit report on file.

Name of Creditor

Account Number

Item Description: *(Use info on the credit report)*

In compliance with the Fair Credit Reporting Act (FCRA), I respectfully request that you investigate my claim. If you discover my claim to be valid and accurate after your investigation is complete, I request for you to {delete, update, correct} the item immediately.

Furthermore, I would like to request for you to send me a corrected copy of my credit report and a list of all the creditors who have received a copy of my credit report within the last 6 months, or the last 2 years for the purposes of employment.

Additionally, I would please ask for you to provide me with the name, address, and telephone number of each credit grantor or other subscriber that has received a copy of my credit report from your company within the past 6 months.

If the outcome of your investigation determines the disputed information is not inaccurate, then please send me a description of the technique used to help you come to this conclusion. Please send this description within 15 days of the completion of your re-investigation, as required by the Fair Credit Reporting Act.

Thank you for your cooperation in this matter. If you have any questions about my request, I can be reached at (insert daytime phone number including area code).

Thank you for your time,
YOUR SIGNATURE
YOUR FIRST AND LAST NAME
YOUR SOCIAL SECURITY NUMBER

Seventh Sample Dispute Letter

Use the following sample dispute letter if your credit report shows an account that you do not recognize.

Credit Bureau Name   Your Name

Credit Bureau Address   Your Address

Credit Bureau City, State, and Zip   Your City, State, Zip
                                                            Your Date of Birth
Date   Your Social Security Number

Dear CREDIT BUREAU NAME,

Re: Account Name and Number

I recently received a free copy of my credit report. Upon reviewing the report, I noticed it contains accounts I don't remember opening before. I have no idea what these accounts are and request they be removed. I am NOT claiming fraud or identity theft - I do not honestly remember.

CREDIT ACCOUNT NAME
      ACCOUNT   NUMBER

When my credit report has been corrected please send a corrected report to me.

Thank you for your time,
YOUR SIGNATURE
YOUR FIRST AND LAST NAME

Eighth Sample Dispute Letter

Use the following sample dispute letter if your credit report shows an account you do not recognize.

Credit Bureau Name	Your Name
Credit Bureau Address	Your Address
Credit Bureau City, State, and Zip	Your City, State, Zip
	Your Date of Birth
Date	Your Social Security Number

Dear CREDIT BUREAU NAME,

Re: Account Name and Number

This letter is to request you to remove inaccurate information from my credit report. Such inaccurate information has affected my chances of getting loans and credit. For your convenience, I have supplied a list of inaccurate accounts below.

ENTER ACCOUNT INFORMATION HERE

I hereby request you to make the changes within 30 days to avoid any violation of the FCRA.

Please send me a copy of the updated credit report at your earliest convenience.

Thank you for your time,

YOUR SIGNATURE

YOUR FIRST AND LAST NAME

Ninth Sample Dispute Letter

Use the following sample dispute letter if your credit report shows an account you do not recognize.

Credit Bureau Name	Your Name
Credit Bureau Address	Your Address
Credit Bureau City, State, and Zip	Your City, State, Zip
	Your Date of Birth
Date	Your Social Security Number

Dear CREDIT BUREAU NAME,

Re: Account Name and Number

I recently received a free copy of my credit report from your service and have found the following items to be erroneous.

CREDITOR NAME

ACCOUNT NUMBER

According to Section 611 of the Fair Credit Reporting Act, I am respectfully requesting for you to investigate the indicated items, and to delete any unverifiable, inaccurate, or outdated information from my credit report as quickly as possible.

I also want to request a description of how the investigation was performed, and the name, address, and telephone number of anyone contacted for information.

Furthermore, if there is a change in my credit history resulting from your investigation, I am requesting that an updated report be sent to those who received my report, within the last two years for employment purposes, or within the last one year for any other purpose.

Please send me a new copy of my updated report, and notification that items have been deleted. I will consider 30 days a reasonable time for your re-verification of these items.

Thank you for your prompt attention in this matter.

Thank you for your time,
YOUR SIGNATURE
YOUR FIRST AND LAST NAME
YOUR SOCIAL SECURITY NUMBER

Tenth Sample Dispute Letter

Use the following sample dispute letter if your credit report shows an account you do not recognize.

Credit Bureau Name   Your Name

Credit Bureau Address   Your Address

Credit Bureau City, State, and Zip   Your City, State, Zip

Your Date of Birth

Date   Your Social Security Number

Dear CREDIT BUREAU NAME,

Re: Account Name and Number

I am contacting you because I found some information that is inaccurate on my credit report.

The date-of-last-activity you are reporting for this account doesn't match my records. I request that you verify the information and remove any inaccurate information from my credit report as quickly as possible. The items in question are:

CREDITOR'S NAME

ACCOUNT NUMBER

After doing so, please provide me with an updated credit report reflecting the changes.

Thank you for your time,

YOUR SIGNATURE

YOUR FIRST AND LAST NAME

Chapter 8 – Advanced Credit Repair Tactics

If you've made it this far in the book, then you know all about sending out dispute letters to credit bureaus so that you can fix the mistakes in your credit reports. The Fair Credit Reporting Act requires credit bureaus to investigate these disputes.

Creditors don't usually like to remove inaccuracies from consumer credit reports, even if they understand the inaccuracies are real and should be removed. You understand why this is the case because of what you learned already. Creditors prefer to have credit reports with lousy information about consumers.

If you want to ensure the most damaging accounts are removed from your credit reports, you need to learn about advanced credit repair tactics. These are not like the disputes you file with the three credit bureaus. Advanced disputes have hundreds of laws that govern them, in addition to the Fair Credit Reporting Act. That is what makes them different.

Advanced disputes are directed more towards the creditors to ensure they're compliant with all the federal laws that govern their conduct. Since creditors make money from your credit report information, they see bigger profits when your credit score is low. They might even go so far as to change data on the report to make it look bad.

If you want to remove inaccurate or invalid debts from your credit report, the law is on your side. More than 200 laws are on the books that protect consumer rights. Don't expect your creditors to care for these laws because they regulate their conduct extensively. But they're willing to break those laws anyway because they're hoping you won't understand your legal rights under those laws.

As you proceed through this chapter, you'll learn about how to write advanced letters to remove the worst accounts from your credit reports. These advanced letters will ensure your creditors remain in compliance with all relevant consumer laws.

An Overview of Advanced Letters

When you initiate an advanced dispute with a creditor, you are basically accusing them of violating specific consumer laws. You have the legal right to request information and documentation from your creditors directly.

Under the Fair Billing Act, you have the right to request billing statements, debt breakdowns, and other relevant documentation from your creditors. They are not allowed to refuse your request. The dispute letter outlines all the options available to the creditor to provide documentation and the consequences of not deleting invalid items from the report.

If you find a creditor has violated the law in how they handled your request, then you can go after them in court for civil penalties. All creditors must store the necessary documentation and provide it to consumers when it is requested. However, they are voluntarily deleting invalid items from your credit report. That is what usually happens with an advanced dispute letter.

There are so many examples of advanced disputes that could be mentioned. For instance, let's say a collection company violated the HIPPA law, and you wanted to challenge the company with an advanced dispute. Perhaps a medical collection was reported that broke numerous medical privacy laws. Advanced dispute tactics will ensure that item is removed from your report.

Creditors are willing to voluntarily delete negative items from credit reports because they're afraid of lawsuits and FTC complaints being filed against them. They are even more afraid of the authorities investigating their conduct in the past and present. Therefore, they would rather delete the negative items to avoid all the legal trouble that could lie ahead if they don't cooperate.

You might be surprised to learn that creditors don't receive too many advanced dispute letters. They make it their mission to find uneducated consumers who don't know their legal rights. The odds are that only 1 out of 400 consumers will actually send an advanced dispute to a creditor. The other 399 consumers won't do anything because they don't' know their options.

It is no big deal for a creditor if they have to cooperate with 1 out of 400 consumers. It is better than facing the threat of a lawsuit or legal problems with the Secretary of State or Federal Trade Commission.

Now that you know the basics of advanced dispute letters and how they function, the next step is to understand the consumer laws so that you can challenge your creditors correctly.

You don't have to choose between advanced dispute letters and formal credit bureau dispute letters. You can work on both at the same time. Just choose the right advanced letter sample to send to your creditor.

Your advanced letter should include your account name, account number, and signature. When you're done describing your dispute in the letter, mail it right to the creditor. You can see the names of each creditor on your credit report. If you need to find their addresses, look at the report from your credit monitoring service or the report your creditors send to you. Those reports should have their addresses on them.

Advanced letters should never get sent to the credit bureaus. They are meant for the creditors only. The difference between the two types of letters is simple. The advanced letters are meant to challenge a creditor by threatening them with legal consequences if they don't remove negative items from your credit report. Regular dispute letters to credit bureaus are merely pointing out the reasons for your disputes. No threats are made here.

After you mail out your dispute letters, update your credit report online periodically. Since the creditors are not legally required to respond to your advanced letters directly, you'll know they got your letter if the negative items appear to be removed from your credit report.

Samples of Advanced Dispute Letters

In this section, you will find samples of advanced dispute letters. Perhaps they can help you get started with your advanced letter writing. These samples might not coincide with your specific problem or situation, so you might need to search online for better samples if needed.

If you need additional assistance, then it is always wise to consult with a professional credit specialist or consumer credit law attorney.

A Simple Request in Good Faith

Creditor Name   Your Name
Creditor Address   Your Address
Creditor City, State, and Zip   Your City, State, Zip
                                                    Your Date of Birth
                               Your Social Security Number

Date

Dear CREDITOR NAME,

Re: Account Name and Number

I am respectfully requesting your help regarding a negative item listed on my credit report. Back in _____, I lost my job and ended up making some late payments because of it. I never wanted to be late but I had no choice because of my financial situation. Fortunately, my financial status has gotten better since then and my account is now current.

All my payments continue to be on time now. I've overcome my hardships to make better decisions with my finances. I feel I have total control of my money and how it is spent and saved.

My current objective is to purchase a home. However, I still have a negative item on my credit report. As a result, I cannot find a low mortgage rate for my loan. If you could please remove the negative item from my credit report out of good faith, I would humbly appreciate it.

Thank you so much for your time and consideration,

YOUR SIGNATURE
YOUR FIRST AND LAST NAME

Validating Debt Under the Fair Billing Act and Fair Debt Collection Practices Act

Creditor Name   Your Name

Creditor Address   Your Address

Creditor City, State, and Zip   Your City, State, Zip

                                                        Your Date of Birth

Date   Your   Social   Security
Number

Dear CREDITOR NAME,

Re: Account Name and Number

The purpose of this letter is to inquire about the accuracy of a debt listed on my credit report. I'm not refusing to pay the debt, but a notice was sent pursuant to the Fair Debt Collection Practices Act, 15 USC 1692g Sec. 809 (b) that your claim is disputed and that validation is requested.

I am not requesting verification of the debt, but rather validation of the debt, pursuant to the above-named Title and Section. I respectfully request that your offices provide me with the proper evidence which proves my legal obligation to pay you the debt allegedly owed.

I would like to know the following information:

- What do I owe the money for?
- Explain how you calculated the money I supposedly owe?
- Show me copies of documentation which indicate that I agreed to undertake the debt or pay the amount owed.
- Show me a verification or copy of a judgement.

- What is the name of the creditor?

- Prove to me the Statute of Limitations has not expired.

- Are you a licensed creditor in the state? If so, show me the proof. What are your license numbers?

At this time, I will also inform you that if your offices have reported invalidated information to any of the 3 major Credit Bureau's (Equifax, Experian or Trans Union) this action might constitute fraud under both Federal and State Laws.

Due to this fact, if any negative mark is found on any of my credit reports by your company or the company that you represent, I will not hesitate in bringing legal action against you for the following:

- Violation of the Fair Credit Reporting Act
- Violation of the Fair Debt Collection Practices Act
- Defamation of Character

If your offices are able to provide the proper documentation as requested in the following Declaration, I will require at least 30 days to investigate this information and during such time all collection activity must cease and desist.

Also, during this validation period, if any action is taken which could be considered detrimental to any of my credit reports, I will consult with my legal counsel for suit. This includes any listing any information to a credit reporting repository that could be inaccurate or invalidated or verifying an account as accurate when in fact there is no provided proof that it is.

If your offices fail to respond to this validation request within 30 days from the date of your receipt, all references to this account must be deleted and completely removed from my credit file and a copy of such deletion request shall be sent to me immediately.

It would be advisable that you assure that your records are in order before I am forced to take legal action. This is an attempt to correct your records; any information obtained shall be used for that purpose.

Thank you for your time,
YOUR SIGNATURE
YOUR FIRST AND LAST NAME

Validating Debt in Accordance with the Fair Debt Collection Practices Act

Creditor Name	Your Name
Creditor Address	Your Address
Creditor City, State, and Zip	Your City, State, Zip
	Your Date of Birth
Date	Your Social Security Number

Dear CREDITOR NAME,

Re: Account Name and Number

I am continually being called on the telephone by your firm over this alleged debt. I'm sure you are aware of the provisions in the Fair Debt Collection Practices Act (FDCPA), and I am requesting validation of this debt.

I am requesting proof that I am indeed the party you are asking to pay this debt, and there is some contractual obligation which is binding on me to pay this debt. I request that you stop contacting us on the telephone and restrict your contact with us to writing, and only when you can provide adequate validation of this alleged debt.

To refresh your memory on what constitutes legal validation, I am giving a list of the required documentation:

- Complete payment history, the requirement of which has been established via Spears v Brennan 745 N.E.2d 862; 2001 Ind. App. LEXIS 509 and
- Agreement that bears the signature of the alleged debtor wherein he agreed to pay the original creditor.
- Letter of sale or assignment from the original creditor to your company. (Agreement with your client that grants you the authority to collect on this alleged debt.) Coppola v. Arrow Financial Services, 302CV577, 2002 WL 32173704 (D.Conn., Oct. 29, 2002) - Information relating to the purchase of a bad debt is not proprietary or burdensome. Debtor must phrase their request clearly to obtain: The source of a debt and the amount a bad debt buyer paid for plaintiff's debt, how amount sought was calculated, where in issue a list of reports to credit bureaus, and documents conferring authority on defendant to collect debt.
- Intimate knowledge of the creation of the debt by you, the collection agency.

I'm sure you know, under FDCPA Section 809 (b), you are not allowed to pursue collection activity until the debt is validated. You should be made aware that in TWYLA BOATLEY, Plaintiff, vs. DIEM CORPORATION, No. CIV 03-0762 UNITED STATES DISTRICT COURT FOR THE DISTRICT OF ARIZONA, 2004, the courts ruled that reporting a collection account indeed is considered collection activity.

While I prefer not to litigate, I will use the courts as needed to enforce my rights under the FDCPA.

I look forward to an uneventful resolution of this matter.

Thank you for your time,
YOUR SIGNATURE
YOUR FIRST AND LAST NAME
YOUR ACCOUNT NUMBER WITH THE CREDITOR

Chapter 9 – Anything but Easy

All of these dispute letters and processes might feel overwhelming to someone new. You have to keep track of so many different letters for various types of disputes. It can get frustrating.

Credit repair is not as simple as it might seem. If you make one little mistake in your dispute, you'll have to wait at least a month to learn about it. But what happens if you don't get a response after a month? What if 2 months goes by and you don't get a response? Maybe your letters never arrived at the credit bureaus' addresses. Should you send more letters out to the credit bureaus?

These are all too common questions people ask themselves after they've sent dispute letters and received no response. If they do get a response, the bureaus might tell you that on inaccuracies were found in your credit reports. That means no changes will be made to the reports.

In addition to dealing with all this stress, you have to think about your credit scores constantly. Credit scores now have the power to stop your employment and prevent you from getting a car loan or mortgage loan. It only takes one late or missing monthly payment on an existing loan to destroy your credit. In fact, you could be late paying your power bill and it'll affect your credit.

All your hopes and dreams rely on good credit. If you want to purchase your dream home or car, you need good credit to get approved for the loan. If you want that dream job that pays six figures per year, you must pass a credit check beforehand. That is why a good credit score has never been more important than in today's society.

This book has given you the knowledge, skills, tools, and letters needed to help you manage your credit score in the best possible ways. But even with all these resources available at your disposal, credit repair is never an easy thing. It is almost like representing yourself as an attorney because it forces you to learn legal terminology and hold creditors accountable for the accuracy of your credit reports.

Remember that people with good credit scores pay lower interest rates on loans. You'll actually end up saving money if you simply manage your credit reports. And if you need more assistance or educational tools to learn this process, the internet has hundreds of tutorial videos and eBooks devoted to the credit services industry.

Transformation is the name of the game. Sometimes it requires a little extra professional help to get you on the right track. A personal coach can teach you the blueprint of credit management and strategizing. If you want to learn each step in repairing your credit so that your credit report is in good standing, then I invite you to take the next steps below.

If you need help with credit restoration we are more than happy to assist you. Just visit us online at www.flournoyfinancial.com

Conclusion

Congratulations. You've made it to the end of the book! You must really understand the importance of good credit. Are you finally ready to take it seriously now?

A positive credit profile is the true path to the American dream. It will allow you to get hired for good jobs and get approved for mortgage loans and car loans with low interest rates.

If you apply for a credit card with a good credit score, you could find yourself with high credit limits and low interest rates. Sometimes the APR is 0% for the first 12 months.

Keep credit lines openly available. You never know when you'll have an emergency expense to face. As you save more money, you can apply it to your retirement, vacation, or business. The sky's the limit.

Are you ready to take control of your credit score? If you've read through all the material in this book, then you're probably feeling pretty confident about your knowledge of the credit system. That is good because now is your chance to apply that knowledge to real life and fix your credit.

Good luck!

Ra'Shawn D. Flournoy

About the Author

Ra'Shawn D. Flournoy is an American entrepreneur, investor, pastor, author and motivational speaker. He is best known as the founder and lead pastor of Movement Church located in Charlotte, North Carolina. In 2017, his partner and himself was homeless, $50,000 in debt, living out of the church and bathing in the public bathrooms. It was then that he made a life-changing decision to re-invent himself and his career. By 2019 at the age of thirty four, Ra'Shawn founded his first funding and credit repair company Flournoy Financial Group. His company now processes thousands of applications each month producing in excess of $1 billion in funding.